Twelfth Man

A comedy

"H" Connolly

Samuel French – London
New York – Sydney – Toronto – Hollywood

CHARACTERS

Billy Wigley, a cocky but likeable young man
Pauline Hincliff, admired by Billy
Len Hincliff, Pauline's dad and the team captain, over-
 bearing and full of self importance; middle-aged
Ray, quiet; middle-aged
Jean Hincliff, Len's long-suffering wife
Duncan, easygoing, accident-prone
Doc, well-spoken, jovial; middle-aged
Jack Digem, local undertaker, a dry old stick with a
 wicked sense of humour
Mary Townsend ⎫
Freda Troutman ⎬ extrovert, sporty young women who
Sally Field ⎭ turn up unexpectedly
Alice, Leroy's mother, a large, middle-aged American

The action of the play takes place in a small cricket
pavilion in Tetford, West Yorkshire

ACT I
SCENE 1 Saturday, 10.30 p.m.
SCENE 2 Early Sunday Afternoon

ACT II
SCENE 1 An hour and a half later
SCENE 2 After tea the same day

ACT I

SCENE 1

A small cricket pavilion in Tetford, West Yorkshire. Saturday, 10.30 p.m.

A modestly furnished hut with a central light and badly patched roof. There is a main entrance UR, to the left of which is a window overlooking the pitch. DL is a door to the changing room and DR is a door to the kitchen. There is a small scoring table under the window and a larger table in the centre of the room. Behind the main door hangs a mirror, above a bench, and to the left of the door there hangs an old cricket bat

As the CURTAIN rises the stage is almost in darkness. In the dim moonlight Billy may be seen as he opens the pavilion door, lets in Pauline, comes in, shuts the door and switches the light on. Pauline crosses to the table and sits down on top of it. She is eating a pickled gherkin

Billy Come on, Pauline. You're not much fun to take on a date.

Pauline Oh, listen to Billy Wigley, the last of the big spenders, takes you out to the pub and buys you two sweet Martinis and a pickled gherkin, then brings you back to the village cricket pavilion with the roof leaking and wonders why a girl doesn't feel romantic!

Billy I can't help that—there's nowhere else to go, is there? We can't go back to my house and your dad's threatened to do me a mischief if he catches me with you again. (*He paces the room*) I've only got the keys to this place because I've got to mark the pitch out in the morning for the game.

Pauline screams and jumps up

What's the matter now?

Pauline A rain drop's gone down the back of my dress.

Billy Lucky rain drop! It's a lot further than I've ever got.

Pauline Very funny!

Billy Here. (*He takes his jacket off and gives it to her*)

Pauline And I've lost my pickled gherkin (*She puts his jacket over her shoulders*)

Billy Good—now that means that I can kiss you good-night later.

Pauline Oh, and what makes you think you're going to be lucky enough to get a good-night kiss? (*She sits back down on the edge of the table*)

Billy (*moving towards her*) I'll just blind you with my irresistible charm and wit (*he bends close to her*) and you'll be like putty in my hands. (*He tries to kiss her*)

Pauline puts the gherkin in her mouth and starts chewing it

Billy You found that bloody gherkin! (*He moves away*)

Pauline Thankfully. It was on the table.

Billy I can't understand you. If you don't like me why did you agree to come up here?

Pauline I never said I didn't like you.

Billy (*looking at her*) Oh.

Pauline It's just that I like gherkins more.

Billy There you go again—building me up then knocking me back down again. I feel like a kiddy's Lego kit.

Pauline (*going to him*) I'm sorry, Billy. I don't mean to—honest. It's just—well I want a bit more from life than most of the girls around these parts. I'd like to travel.

Billy Now you sound like one of them dozy tarts in a beauty contest. (*In a funny voice*) "And I'd like to travel and see the world and be kind to animals . . ." (*He turns to her*) What's wrong with Yorkshire, that's what I'd like to know? It's been good enough for six generations of your family, or so your dad keeps telling everyone.

Pauline So he does. (*She sits on the table*) We had an uncle from me mum's side—he moved from Yorkshire to live in Bolton—years ago this was—but from the day he left, our dad wouldn't talk to him. Me uncle used to write us letters and send us Christmas cards and Dad would rip them up without even opening them. He'd rant on about him being a traitor and going over to the enemy. You'd have thought he was Lord Haw-Haw!

Billy Well no-one ever said the Wars of the Roses were over.

Pauline (*jumping up from the table*) You're as bad as the rest.

Billy Look Pauline, I'll tell you something now but I don't want you to breathe a word to a living soul.

Pauline My—I'm right intrigued.

Billy I've had some scouts round our place talking to me dad. They've been pestering him for days.

Pauline It's probably "bob a job" week.

Billy Not bloody boy scouts!

Pauline What then?

Billy Cricket scouts.

Pauline Cricket! (*She turns and walks away*)

Billy Well, I was voted best young slow left-arm bowler in West Yorkshire last season.

Pauline So you keep telling me.

Billy They say I've got an unplayable googly.

Pauline Well, I'll have to take your word for that one, won't I!

Billy They've been round our house asking me dad if I'd go for trials.

Pauline If you wanted to make a fool of yourself prancing around a field dressed all in white, you should have been a morris dancer.

Billy You don't like cricket, do you?

Pauline No I don't!

Billy But your dad lives for cricket.

Pauline That may have something to do with why I don't like it.

Billy You won't tell him, will you?

Pauline That I don't like cricket? I think he already knows.

Billy No! That I'm going for trials. He's still very bitter about what happened to him twenty years ago when he was asked to—mind you, he was a great fast bowler in his day.

Pauline We get that everytime that man comes on telly, "I could have played for England if it hadn't been for him".

Billy Your dad was just unlucky that he was at his prime when Yorkshire had one of the best fast bowlers of all time—Fiery Fred Truman. What a sight to behold, running in with his shirt sleeve flapping in the wind and hair flopping all over the shop.

Pauline When I was a girl and everyone used to go on about Fiery Fred, I used to think they were talking about an arsonist. (*She sits*)

Billy Your dad was heartbroken when that dodgy knee of his stopped him playing for Yorkshire.

Pauline The only thing that stopped him playing for Yorkshire was that he wasn't good enough!

Billy (*turning to her*) Maybe if I made the grade in these trials, it would make up for some of his disappointment. It's his captaincy that's made me what I am.

Pauline Yes. He's a lot to answer for, has Dad.

Billy So if you married me and Yorkshire signed me up, you would be able to travel.

Pauline What! To Headingly!—I can get to Headingly with a fifty pence bus ride. I was thinking of travelling a bit further than that.

Billy No, I'd be on the county circuit.

Pauline Yes and I'd be on Valium!

Billy You'd be all right—I'd be famous.

Pauline Can't you see, cricket doesn't interest me—I don't want to be like me mam and spend twenty years making crab paste sandwiches every Sunday for the whole of the summer.

Billy Every other Sunday.

Pauline What?

Billy We play away every other week, so you'd only make sandwiches for home games.

Pauline Oh, shut up! I'm not making your silly sandwiches, nor am I working in that sewing factory until I'm too old and they kick me out. (*She screams and jumps up again*)

Billy What's the matter?

Pauline Bloody rain drop again.

Billy Let's hope it stops for morning. It's an important game tomorrow.

Pauline Shouldn't you be home in bed.

Billy Pauline, that's a great idea. Come on!

Pauline I mean resting before the big match, not be out here all night drinking beer and trying to bowl a maiden over.

Billy I thought you didn't know anything about cricket.

Pauline I said I didn't like it—you can't grow up in our house without learning something about cricket.

Car headlights flash across the window. Billy runs over to the light switch and turns it off

Hey, don't you start getting any funny ideas.

Billy No! Someone's coming. I saw the car headlights as they turned off the road.

They go to the window—the headlights come nearer. They run back

Pauline Oh no! Lord help us if we get caught. My dad will thrash me.

Billy Worse than that—he'll thrash me an' all.

Pauline Can we make a run for it?

Billy No, they'd pick us up in their lights.

Pauline What are we going to do?

Billy Hide!

Pauline Where?

Billy Under the table.

They dive under the table as the headlights shine right in the window. Two car doors shut and footsteps are heard coming to the door. There is the sound of the door being unlocked

Len and Ray come in. They are both wearing raincoats and flat caps

Len Don't touch the switch. (*He walks to the light bulb and touches it. It burns his hand but he tries not to show it*) Just as I thought—someone's been here, the light bulb's still hot.

Ray (*putting the light on*) I thought I could see a light from the road as we came in. (*He moves near the door to the changing rooms*)

Len It's the yobos from the village again. Some parents have got no idea what their kids are up to, long as their out of their hair—no discipline, Ray, that's the problem with 'em these days.

Ray You're probably right, Len.

Len Let's look in the changing rooms.

Ray What for?

Len They may still be in there.

Ray (*his face dropping*) You think so? (*He moves away from the door*)

Len (*picking up an old cricket bat from the back wall and crossing* UC) I hope so. (*He holds the bat up*) I'll bounce the buggers round the walls.

Ray But what if there's a lot of them?

Len Where's your backbone, man?

Ray I think I left it in the car.

Len Ay, the same place you leave it in the game when their fast bowler comes back on.

Len exits through the changing room door pushing Ray before him

Pauline (*from under the table*) It's my dad! What are we going to do? He'll kill me if he finds us here.

Billy I know! (*He thinks*) Still, I'm supposed to be here to mark out the pitch.

Pauline Yes, in the morning you are! You can't mark a pitch out in the middle of the night.

Billy We'd better try an' sneak out while they're in the changing rooms.

They both crawl around one end of the table, each going towards the door, but a noise from the changing rooms sends them back under the table

  Len and Ray enter

Len They must have heard us coming and run out the back way.

Ray Good!

Len What do you mean "good"? We need to catch one of the little sods and give 'em the thrashing of their life; it will frighten the other beggars off. (*He hits the bat down on the table*)

Billy and Pauline jump

Ray It's not really the kids' fault. They've got no place to go, since the youth ... (*He looks at Len*)

Len Say it, man. If you've got something on your mind let's have it out.

Ray I was only saying since the youth club got knocked down, there's no place for them to go at nights.

Len And I suppose that's my fault.

Ray No, not really. The youth club was on your land and you're free to sell it to the highest——

Len stares at him

—sell it to who you like.

Len Progress, Ray—we can't stand in the way of progress.

Ray If you say so.

Len I do. (*He picks something up from the table*) What do you make of that?

Ray looks

Ray It's half a pickled gherkin.

Pauline puts her hand to her mouth. Len and Ray move to the front of the table

What's it doing here?

Len You'd be surprised what you find lying about in here. (*He turns and looks at Ray*) You was umpiring some of that game two Sundays ago, wasn't you?

Ray Yes, early on I done a spell.

Len Didn't you find it?

Ray What?

Len In the umpire's coat pocket.

Ray I don't follow.

Len When I took the umpire's coat after you that week, I put me hand in the pocket and there it was.

Ray What?

Len The anti-baby implement.

Ray looks shocked

   Thankfully still in its wrapper.

Ray Oh?

Len One of them froggy notes.

Ray looks blank

   A condom!

Ray (*hastily*) It wasn't mine!

Len I didn't think for one minute it was. The coat's left on peg in changing rooms all week. One of the village yobos that get in here at nights must have put it in the pocket for a joke.

Ray I suppose they must have done.

Len But you must have found it in pocket when you was umpiring?

Ray (*nervously*) I remember finding something but I thought it was a plaster.

Len A plaster!

Ray I didn't pay much attention.

Len I did. It was most embarrassing when I went to put the bails back on the stumps after tea. That froggy note fell out on the floor. Everyone saw it and their wag of a captain shouted, "It don't look like the umpire's going to get caught out this afternoon, lads!"

Ray It was only a bit of fun.

Len Yes, fun at my expense—I don't like being made a fool of. (*Moving towards Ray*) That's why I got you up here, so we could talk and not be disturbed.

Ray (*nervously*) Talk? About what?

Len I've noticed one or two things lately—things that I don't like the look of.

Ray W—W—What's this to do with me, Len?

Len There's got to be some changes. (*He moves closer to Ray*) Things can't go on as they are—people are starting to notice.

Ray T—They are?

Len I tell you, Ray, I'm not frightened to swing the axe when things get tough.

Ray Axe! (*He runs his finger around his collar*)

Len So that's why I brought you up here (*he leans towards Ray*) out of the way, so it's nice and quiet, no-one around to hear.

Ray (*nervously*) Have you talked to your wife about this?

Len I did mention it to her, but she wasn't very interested.

Ray She wasn't?

Len Told me to do what I thought best.

Ray (*in a high voice*) She did!

Len She's more worried about what to put in the sandwiches tomorrow.

Ray She is.

Len Told me to make whatever changes I thought best.

Ray Changes?

Len To the team. I'm swinging the axe on one or two players for tomorrow's game.

Ray (*relieved*) Oh, I see. The team. You're dropping some players.

Len Yes.

Ray Couldn't you have told me that in the pub?

Len No—too many ears in that place. I want this kept secret till morning.

Ray Who are you dropping?

Len Only two players—we've not been starting off the batting very well lately. We've been bogged down early on, so I'm dropping one of our openers.

Ray But you open the batting with Bob Tiler.

Len Ay, so I'm dropping Bob.

Ray Dropping Bob? But he topped the averages last year.

Len That was last year.

Ray But he made fifty last week—(*he looks at Len*)—well he would have made fifty if he hadn't been run out.

Len Are you accusing me of getting him run out.

Ray No.

Len I distinctly heard him shout for that second run.

Ray He shouted "No!"—everyone in ground heard it!

Len From where I was standing it sounded like "Go"—anyway, he'd have made it if he was faster between wickets.

Ray He'd have had to have been a whippet.

Len What?

Ray I said it's a funny game cricket.

Len There's nowt funny about it. It's deadly serious—especially tomorrow's match. It's against a team of southern pansies. They'll never be able to play cricket down south. Their hands are too soft to hold a bat properly.

Ray They beat us last year.

Len That's because I retired hurt.

Ray Yes, you broke a finger trying to catch the ball.

Len It would have been the catch of the season if I'd held it.

Ray You pushed it over the boundary for a six.

Len Never mind that!

Ray Anyway, it's not the same team this year. They couldn't fit us in.

Len Cheek!

Ray takes a letter from his pocket

Ray So they've asked another team if they could fit us in. It's in a letter I got from Steventon's secretary. Do you remember him?

They look at each other

Oh, of course you do, it was him that bust your finger.

Len (*grabbing the letter*) Yes, I've read the letter as well. We're playing W.W.C.C.

Ray Who are they?

Len According to Steventon's secretary, it's Whitney West Indian Cricket Club. Their captain's wife phoned last night to see if everything was all right.

Ray Oh no! A West Indian team! That means at least four fast bowlers.

Len Ay, but there's some of us that can fire the ball up round their lug-holes, if they want to play silly beggars.

Ray Yes, I do believe young Harry Clegg's getting faster every year.

Len He may be getting faster, but I'm the most accurate. Took more wickets than any opening bowler in West Yorkshire last season.

Ray That was last season.

Len What do you mean?

Ray You only took more wickets because you bowled twice as many overs as anybody else—you never knew when to take yourself off.

Len I can't help it if I've got stamina.

Ray It's not stamina—it's stubbornness. Remember that game last season, you bowled so much you collapsed with exhaustion.

Len It were sunstroke.

Ray Sunstroke! We played in the rain all day because you wouldn't call the game off.

Len It didn't rain all day!

Ray It did. You may have collapsed with 'flu, but it sure as heck wasn't sunstroke. Anyway, who's the second one you're axing? Me I suppose.

Len Nay.

Ray I wouldn't mind if you did. Them West Indian boys can throw the ball down track a bit too fast for my liking.

Len I'm not dropping you—maybe you can't bat or bowl, but you're the only one silly enough to stand behind stumps and keep wicket.

Ray Everyone's got to be good at something.

Len No, it's young Billy Wigley I'm dropping.

Billy jumps and hits his head on the table

Ray What was that?

Len Oh, I don't know—the place is full of rats.

Ray (*looking at him*) Ay ... Why are you dropping young Billy? He's best young slow bowler I've seen in years. They say Yorkshire's watching him.

Len (*moves away from him* R) Don't be daft! He'll never be good enough to play for Yorkshire and I should know.

Ray Yes, I suppose you would!

Len He's getting too big for his boots. Do him good to be brought down a peg or two. So Billy will start off as twelfth man and Duncan will play in his place.

Ray Have you told him?

Ray Ay, I told Duncan early on.

Ray No! Young Billy, have you let him know?

Len Well, not yet. I've not had a chance—I'll tell him in the morning before game starts.

Ray But he's mowing the grass and marking pitch out in the morning.

Len It's all right, a bit of hard work never hurt a young lad, and anyway he'll have to get used to it if he's going to play for Yorkshire.

Ray I thought he wasn't good enough.

Len (*shouting*) He ain't and don't try to get me annoyed. (*He moves to the door*) Let's go. I've left the car lights on and I don't want the battery going flat on me. (*He switches off the lights to the pavilion*)

Ray I can't see where I'm going!

Len Well, open they bloody eyes then.

Ray stumbles to the door

They exit

The room remains in darkness except for the dim light from the car headlights

Pauline Have they gone?

Billy Shh! Hang on.

The sound of a car trying to start up is heard. On the third turn it starts and they drive off

Pauline Get off!

Billy I'm looking for my torch.

Pauline Well, you won't find it down there!

Billy It's in my jacket pocket and you're wearing my jacket.

Pauline Hang on. (*She gives him the torch*)

He turns the torch on and goes over to the light switch. He switches it on. Pauline crawls from under the table. They both start stretching

Pauline I thought they was going to talk all night.

Billy They've dropped me!

Pauline What's the matter?

Billy Your dad's dropped me!

Pauline He will if he catches you out with me. I've got to get home before he does.

Billy It's all right we'll take the short cut along the canal.

Pauline But the path's covered in mud and I've got my best shoes on.

Billy Well, take them off then.

Pauline Thank you Sir Galahad!

He grabs her hand and opens the door

Don't forget the lights, dope!

He switches off the light

They both exit

CURTAIN

SCENE 2

The same. Early Sunday afternoon

The pavilion door opens and Len comes in UR *smartly dressed in his best cricket gear. He is carrying one end of a cricket kit-bag. Jean, his wife, follows him in. She is carrying the other end and a large shopping bag*

Len Stop moaning, woman. It could have been worse—at least it's not raining.

Jean If it were raining, I wouldn't have needed to have walked across that mud path by the canal.

They put the kit-bag down

Len It's not my fault the car wouldn't go. You must have flooded it when you tried to start it this morning.

Jean I tell you the battery was flat. (*She puts the shopping bag on the table*)

Len It is now, after you run it into ground. It wouldn't even go with a push.

Jean I'm sorry! I was pushing as fast as I could.

Len You didn't expect me to push it—not with me cricket gear on.

Jean takes her shoe off and looks at it

Jean My heel's come loose.

Len Bloody silly shoes to wear for pushing a car.

Jean I wasn't expecting to have to when I got dressed this morning. (*She hits the heel of the shoe on a bench then puts it back on*)

Len I've got our Pauline to charge the battery. She's going to bring the car up later. (*He looks at her*) You're starting to take a lot of time and trouble getting ready for a game of cricket these days.

Jean No more than you. (*She looks in the shopping bag*)

Len But I'm the captain.

Jean And I'm the tea-lady!

Len I carry a lot of responsibility.

Jean And I carry a lot of teas. (*She puts a box from the bag in his hands*)

Len What's this?

Jean Loo blocks.

Len What for?

Jean Men's toilets. I walked past them the other day and it smelt higher than a kiddy's kite.

Len Can't you see to it, Jean?

Jean No, I can't. I've got to do the sandwiches.

She picks up the shopping bag and goes out to the kitchen

Duncan enters

Duncan Oh, hallo Skip. What you got there?

Len Blocks to you, Duncan!

Duncan Sorry, I was only asking, no need to be so touchy.

Len No Duncan—look, there's something I want you to do for me.

Duncan I know. Bowl.

Len Yes—(*he gives Duncan the box*)—all of them, mind and stick two or three in the urinals.

Duncan What!

Len Gents' loo blocks. (*He pats the box*)

Duncan I meant you wanted me to bowl today instead of young Billy, that's what you said last night.

Len Yes . . . yes, that's right but first of all, can you put a couple of them in toilets. (*He walks away*) I've got to find my team. (*He turns back to him*) I walked past them last week and I noticed they were smelling a bit.

Duncan It was probably Bob Tiler. You can't hit fifty-odd runs in an hour without ponging a bit under the arms.

Len I'm talking about gents' toilets! Get in there and stick a few of them blocks in strategic places.

Duncan exits with the box through the changing room door

Len Score book—I bet she's forgotten the score book again. (*He goes to the kitchen door*)

Doc comes through the outside door. He has an upper-class southern accent

Doc I'm sorry I'm late, Skipper. Mrs Grumshaw's expecting a baby and it wasn't sure if it wanted to be in or out this morning. In the end it was out leg before.

Len (*look at him*) Leg before wicket?

Doc No. Leg before head. It was a breech birth. (*He wanders around the room*) I haven't seen any of the others.

Len What's the woman having, a litter?!

Doc No! Other team members—I thought I was overdue, but it appears I'm premature.

Len Doc, will you stop going on about work, I own the only butchers in town, but I don't talk shop all day.

Doc No—sorry, Skipper—when you look at it we're in the same line of business really.

Len looks at him. Doc laughs to himself

Rain's stopped anyway.

Duncan comes out from the changing rooms

Duncan I've done that little job, Skip. (*Seeing Doc*) Oh, hallo, Doc.

Doc Hallo, Duncan.

Duncan What do you want me to do with the rest of the box?

Len Don't tempt me, Duncan.

Duncan You what?

Len You've only done half a job, as yet.

Duncan No. I've put a block everywhere.

Len But there's the ladies as well!

Duncan has a look of horror on his face

Duncan I couldn't! I'd be too embarrassed. I wouldn't know where to look.

Len Then it's about time you learnt.

Duncan What if someone came in?

Len There's no ladies here.

Duncan Your wife is.

Len Yes, but she doesn't count and anyway, she's making sandwiches.

Duncan (*going over to Doc*) Couldn't you do it—they wouldn't mind with you being a doctor an' all that.

Duncan gives the box to Doc. Len comes over, takes the box from Doc and gives it to Duncan

Len Just get on with it and stop moaning.

Duncan exits to the changing rooms

I've got to find score book.

Len exits to the kitchen

Doc walks over to the mirror on the wall, looks in it, slicks back his hair, straightens his cravat, picks up the old cricket bat and goes through a few practice shots

Duncan comes back from the changing rooms

Doc That was quick work, Duncan. .

Duncan I wasn't going to hang around in there.

Doc I don't suppose anything gets to hang in there.

Duncan There's a lot more writing on the wall than in the gents—that must be because they have a spare hand!

Doc I'd better put my eyes in if I'm going to try and play cricket (*He moves up to the mirror, takes a box from his pocket, and starts putting his contact lenses in*)

Duncan watches open mouthed

Duncan Bit of a tricky job that, Doc.

Doc Not when you get used to it, just needs a steady hand.

Duncan (*watching*) Wouldn't be no good trying to do it after a skin full of Yorkshire bitter. They'd end up half way up your nose!

Doc (*still putting them in*) There's no point putting them in if you've got a hangover, because even if you do manage to find the eye (*he turns to him*) everything still looks blurred. (*The door flies open hits Doc in the back. He throws his arms out and stands blinking*)

Jack enters, dressed in his undertaker's suit, with Ray. He shuts the door

Jack Sorry, Doc. Didn't see you hiding behind door. (*Turning to Ray*) I always told him I'd save him something special for his day of calling. A lovely bit of walnut that was—it's just a pity he couldn't see it.

Ray There's no-one can say you don't get good workmanship from Digem and Sons.

Jack You've got to look after your regulars, haven't you?

Ray Jack—how many regulars does an undertaker get?

Jack A lot relatively speaking.

Duncan You've blinded him!

Ray Who?

Duncan Doc, he was putting his eyes in and you two knocked them out on floor.

Jack (*looking down*) What colour was they?

Doc It's one of my contact lenses that's dropped out, it's just a clear bit of plastic—stand back (*He gets on his knees trying to find it*) It could have gone anywhere

Ray gets on his knees to help

Ray I've heard of a roving eye but this is ridiculous!

All get down on their knees

Len and Jean enter from the kitchen

Len What's going on?

Jean Either they're praying for a win, or we've got them ants back again.

Doc I've lost my contact lens, Skipper. It's on the floor—now everyone stand up.

They all stand up

Now take a big step away

Everyone steps away

Now all move to the middle of the room

All move C

Jean Oh good! A game of "Simon Says"!

Doc The only way to find a lost contact lens is to get the nozzle of a hoover and cover it with a stocking. Then switch the hoover on and the lens will stick to the stocking.

Len There's a hoover out back.

Ray Yes and Jean wears stockings.

She looks at him. They all look at her

Len Come on, lass, it's for the team.

Jean turns to go

Where are you going?

Jean Well you don't think I'm taking my stockings off with you lot watching, do you.

She exits to the kitchen

Len (*to Doc*) It's only you southern softies that has bad eyes. You don't see many Yorkshire folk wearing glasses.

Doc That's because they can't get them on because of the blinkers. (*He starts laughing but sees Len isn't so he stops*) I'm sorry, Skipper. I feel such a fool losing my lens like that.

Len Ay. Well make sure it doesn't happen again.

Noise from off

Duncan Can you hear that rumbling.
Jack Well, it wasn't me this time.
Duncan No, listen.

Everyone listens. The rumbling gets nearer

Doc Oh my God!

The door flies open

> *Billy comes in pulling a small hand roller. He stops it right on the spot where the contact lens fell out. He sees everyone*

Billy Morning! It's quite a nice day for it now.

Everyone stands open-mouthed looking at him

> What's wrong? Has somebody died?

No answer

> No, they can't of—Jack ain't smiling!
Len What are you doing with that little roller!
Billy I'm using it for a paper weight!
Len Why the little one in here?
Billy Because I can't push the big heavy one on me own. I'm using this one to roll the bowler's foot marks.
Doc You've flattened it!
Billy I thought that was the whole idea of rolling it.

Doc takes his handkerchief out and rubs it round the roller

> What's he doing, polishing it?
Jack No, his contact lens has fallen on the floor and you've just pushed the roller over it.
Billy Oh, I see.
Jack Ay, and that's more than he can.
Billy (*excitedly*) If he can't see he won't be able to play! (*He starts to pull the roller out*)
Len Don't move it till we've found his eye!

Everyone gets on their hands and knees except Doc who sits down in a chair C. *He puts his hand in his trouser turn-ups and finds the lens*

Doc It's all right! I've found it—it was caught in my trouser turn-ups.
Billy (*walking away fed up*) The only thing he's caught all bloody season— can I put the roller away now?
Len Leave it outside. You've done enough damage with it already.

> *Jean comes back in carrying a stocking*

Jean (*to Len*) Here you are.
Len What?
Jean You wanted a stocking, didn't you?

Jack takes the stocking from her

Jack It's still warm!

Len (*taking it from him and giving it back to Jean*) We don't need it now. We've found it.

Jean You lot never know what you do want and that's the truth.

She exits to kitchen

Len (*turns to Ray*) How did you know my wife wears stockings?

Ray Ah, yes. Well, you see, I've seen them on washing line as I walked past your house on Monday.

Len Pervert!

Ray We've all got to have a hobby.

Len How do you know that they're not our Pauline's?

Billy No!

Len looks at Billy who quickly moves to the roller

I'll take this out if we've all finished with it, shall I?

He exits with the roller

Ray Have you told Billy he's twelfth man?

Len No, I've not had a chance.

Ray He was just stood right next to you.

Len The time wasn't right—it needs to be done with a bit of subtlety and tact . . .

Ray You mean you'll tell him after he's cut and rolled the pitch.

Jack Are you saying you've dropped young Billy?

Len Yes I have and playing Duncan. Any objections?

Jack No, I'm quite glad really.

Len You see, at last someone in the team can see my thinking on the game and understand my reasons. (*He puts his arm around Jack*)

Jack No, it's not that, I think you're bloody silly not to play the lad. He can bowl people out with his hands in his pockets stood one legged on an orange box, but the thing is he takes same size boots as me, and as mine are a bit worn . . .

Doc A bit worn! They used your boots to knock the stumps in with when Bradman was a boy.

Len I won't have you using that name in this pavilion—he's one of them you know.

Doc I'm sure that's news to Mrs Bradman.

Len No, he's from down there. (*He points to the floor*)

Ray Most Australians do tend to come from that area.

Jack I've put a few Yorkshire men down there as well, in me time—not as far down as Australia mind.

They all stand looking at the floor

Billy enters and sees them

Billy Oh no, Doc's not dropped his contact lens again, has he?

Jean comes in from the kitchen and crosses to the kit-bag

Ray No, it's all right. We're just burying Bradman.

Len Bloody convict!

Jean Do you have to use foul language all the time?

Len When discussing Australians, foul language is the only kind you can use—I can't stand 'em.

Jean I've noticed—he wouldn't even let me take *Crocodile Dundee* out on video!

Jean takes one end of the kit-bag and Ray the other and they exit into the changing room

Len My dad said it's because of all the scraps we had with 'em during the war.

Duncan I know I'm a bit young to remember but weren't they supposed to be on our side!

Len They was, only someone forgot to tell Aussies. Dad said they had more chips on their shoulders than the local French casino.

Jack Talking of things on your shoulders, I've got to go and take the late Terry Sims's coffin to the chapel of rest before the game. Then I've got to go and pick up my sister-in-law.

Len I'm sorry Jack, I didn't know your sister-in-law had died. It won't affect your game, will it?

Jack I doubt it. I've only got to pick her up from train station. She's over here from America on holiday.

Jean enters from the changing room

Len Damn Yanks. Dad didn't like them in the war neither.

Jean Len! It seems the only people your dad got on with during the war was the Germans!

Jean goes out to the kitchen

Len Germans was all right—at least you could shoot at Jerry, Dad said.

Ray comes back in

Jack They're here for a month. The wife's made me take whippets out of front room and lock 'em in shed.

Len They?

Jack Yes. She's brought her son over with her.

Doc Your nephew.

Jack Ay, I suppose he is.

Len You will be back before the start of game, won't you?

Jack Yeah, should be—it depends how much luggage she brings this time. (*To Billy*) Have you cleaned your boots, lad?

Billy Ay, they're as white as a vicar's bum in a nudist camp.

Jack Good. I like to look smart when I'm playing.

Jack goes out

Billy looks at him

Ray If I was a believer in reincarnation, I'd say Jack would have come back as a penguin.

Doc Why's that?

Ray Well, he spends all week in black as an undertaker and the weekends dressed in white playing cricket—no wonder his wife hasn't got a colour telly.

Len You don't half talk some tripe sometimes. Where's the rest of my team.

Billy They're out in the nets practising.

Len Well at least some of 'em are showing some dedication.

Billy I've been trying to get the mower to work but it don't seem to want to go.

Doc Have you put any petrol in it?

Billy Petrol?

Doc Yes, for the engine.

Billy Engine? What engine, I've been pushing the bloody thing all morning.

Len Don't you start getting as silly as him. (*He points to Ray*)

Billy Of course I've put petrol in. I'm not simple you know. I've pulled that starting cord so many times I've gone dizzy!

Len Get Duncan to have a look at it. He's good with engines.

Duncan Right, OK skip.

Billy and Duncan go out

Ray I'll have a look an' all, it's a beast of a thing once it does start.

Ray goes out

Len Doc, I wonder if I could ask your opinion.

Doc (*his eyes light up*) Skipper, it's the first time you've ever asked for my opinion before a game.

Len No. It's your professional opinion I wanted. It's me shoulder, you see—its been playing me up for quite a while.

Doc Oh.

Len Yes. I didn't want to say anything in front of the lads in case they gets despondent before the game. You see, it's effecting me bowling.

Doc You've looked all right the last couple of weeks. The arm's been coming over nicely.

Len It's all a front though, Doc. I've been in agony.

Doc You should have told me. I could have given you some pills for it.

Len I don't need no pills. It's the pain that keeps me going.

Doc Then I can't see what the problem is.

Len The problem is I'm not getting the wickets I should be, with the pain being so bad. I can't make it swing away like I used to—I've lost me best ball.

Doc Yes, that does sound serious.

The sound of a lawn mower trying to start from outside

Len Couldn't you have a quick look? See if you couldn't put it right?

Doc I suppose I could—which shoulder is it?

Len The one that's holding me bowling arm on, fool!

Doc Well, slip your shirt off then.
Len What here?
Doc Yes.
Len It's a bit embarrassing.
Doc Don't be silly. I've seen hundreds of shoulders.

Sound of the lawn mower trying to start again

Len No. Its a personal problem.
Doc Oh that's all right. I'll hold my breath.
Len You don't understand, Doc. I've got a tattoo on my arm.
Doc Believe it or not, I've seen a few of those in me time as well.
Len This tattoo has got a heart with the words "Snuggle bum loves Alice" under it.
Doc But your wife's name's Jean.
Len I know, that's the problem. I had it done before I met her. Some foreign student from Leeds University.
Doc Oh, I see.
Len I was only a lad and she was in her final year. We had a drunken dirty weekend in Scarborough. Then she got homesick and I got the tattoo.
Doc What happened to her?
Len Don't know, never saw her again.
Doc You, I presume, are "Snuggle bum".
Len (*embarrassed*) That's what she called me. Now how can a Yorkshire man walk around with "Snuggle bum" wrote on his arm?
Doc But your wife must have seen it before. You've been married twenty years.
Len I've been very careful about it.
Doc But she must have seen it when you got undressed at night.
Len I always put light off.
Doc You must have taken your shirt off in front of her at some time.
Len Ay, but I've always worn a long sleeved vest.
Doc You've worn a long sleeved vest for twenty years?
Len Not the same one.
Doc You can get them removed by laser now these days.
Len There's no-one pointing one of those things at me arm. I'd rather stick with the vest.
Doc You'll have to take it off so I can look at your shoulder.
Len What, here?
Doc It's as good a place as any. Your wife's out in the kitchen making the sandwiches.
Len Oh, all right but I'm only taking the one arm out. (*He undoes his shirt and sits on the chair*)

From outside the sound of the mower trying to start again. Then there is the sound of the mower being hit

What do you think, Doc?
Doc (*looking*) He's spelt Alice wrong.
Len What?

Doc Only joking! Can you lift your arm up

Len lifts his arm

I need to get some leverage on it. Lay on your stomach over that table.

He does as he is told. Doc rubs his shoulder for a bit. He gets a chair, stands on it then puts his knee on the shoulder and bends the arm back

I want you to tell me if you feel it click (*He pulls the arm*)
Len No

Doc pulls again

... no

He pulls again

no ... no ... no ... no

Jean comes in from the kitchen and sees them

Jean What's this? Two falls, two submissions or a knockout to decide the winner

Doc jumps off Len's back as Len quickly puts his arm back in the vest. He finishes dressing

Doc Ah, you see, it's Len's shoulder. It's giving him a lot of pain.
Jean I'm not surprised, the way you was bending it.
Doc No, I was trying to fix it.
Jean He never said anything to me about it.
Doc Well, you know what these Yorkshire men are like when it comes to pain—it's a tattoo subject—I mean taboo subject—yes.
Jean How is it now, dear?
Len Oh, much better. (*He tries to move it—it isn't*)
Jean Would you like me to have a look at it?
Len No! No it's nothing that a drop of horse linament won't put right.
Doc It's good for sprains is horse linament.
Jean It's like going to bed with Red Rum. One thing about it when you put it on at cricket, it keeps the flies off the teas.
Len Is that what you came in to tell us?
Jean No, I've just seen the opposition's coach pull up from the kitchen window. I thought you'd like to know.

She goes into kitchen

Len (*moving to Doc*) How do I look, Doc?
Doc Do you want my professional opinion again?
Len No, for meeting the opposition's captain. (*He puffs his chest out*) I like to make a good first impression. Try and get the upper hand straight away.
Doc You're so egotistical!
Len It's nice of you to say so. I do try me best ... you watch me take the wind out of their captain's sails when he comes through the door.

Doc It's only a cricket match. Not a yacht race around Cowes.

They both stand waiting

The door opens and three women walk in dressed in tracksuits

Len What do you lasses want?
Sally This is the pavilion, isn't it?
Len Yes, this is the cricket pavilion.
Sally Good, for a minute I thought it was a chicken coop.
Doc The hockey changing rooms are at the other end of the playing fields.
Freda (*looking around*) It's a bit of a dump. I don't think I've ever stripped off in such a small place before.
Sally Don't tell me you never had a boyfriend that owned a mini?
Freda Just my luck, they all did!
Sally I'm talking about cars, dear.
Mary All right, girls. Don't embarrass the opposition.
Len Opposition?
Mary This is Tetford Cricket Club, isn't it?
Len Yes.
Mary Then you are the opposition.
Doc But who are you?
Freda We are your opposition

Len looks at Doc

Len You can't be. We're supposed to be playing Whitney West Indian Cricket Club.
Sally No your not. You're playing Whitney Women's Cricket Club.
Mary On a cricket tour of Yorkshire, whipping the butts of the natives on the pitch and drinking them under the table off it, and I'm the captain— but only because I can drink most and I own the whip.

Doc and Len look totally baffled

Now if one of you boys could point me in the direction of your captain, we could get started.
Doc It's this becalmed gentleman over here.
Mary (*shaking his hand*) Hallo Skip, I'm Mary Townsend.
Len B—But we can't play you, I mean, look at you, you're lasses.
Sally His memory's quite good for an old one.
Len Old one!
Freda And his hearing.
Doc You must excuse us, but we were expecting a team of West Indian gentlemen. It's been advertised in the local press as Trinidad comes to Tetford. We've even got a steel band to play in the tea interval.
Mary I think I know what's happened. Aren't we a rearranged game—you were supposed to play Steventon.
Len Yes but they backed out.
Mary But knowing we were up here on tour they asked us to fulfil the fixture.

Len But their secretary definitely told us you were West Indian and male. The wife's even done a curry goat dip to go with the sandwiches.

Sally That Steventon fixture secretary's got a wicked sense of humour.

Freda He's stitched you up.

Doc Yes, he didn't tell us we would be playing a team of ladies.

Sally You're not.

Mary Don't you remember I phoned you to confirm if the game was on.

Len Yes, but I thought you were the captain's wife passing on a message.

Mary Bit of a mix up all round. What are we going to do?

Doc Well, as you have made the effort to get here, we might as well play the game.

Mary Good. My girls are in the nets already.

Len We most certainly are not playing.

Sally Why not?

Len How can we play against a team of lasses—we'd have to find a tennis ball or something.

Mary No you won't—we have played before. We were unbeaten last season.

Len That was with other lasses. When I'm flat out I've been known to nearly kill a man.

Sally Haven't we all, lovey!

Freda He's talking about bowling, dear.

Mary We have faced fast bowling before and we've got one or two of our own. (*She puts her hand on Freda's shoulder*)

Freda I have been known to shatter the odd stump or two.

Mary This is Freda Troutman, our main strike bowler and this is——

Len (*in disbelief*) Freda Troutman!

Doc Is it a joke?

Freda No.

Len Sacrilege. How dare you come up here poking fun at Fred Truman, the best fast bowler ever to put a shine on a cricket ball.

Freda I'm not. Both my parents are German but I was born in England so I took up one of your national sports.

Len If your parents was krauts, why didn't you take up their national sport?

Doc They haven't got one.

Len Yes they have, it's called war.

Mary OK. So she's a fast bowler with a name that sounds like an old Yorkshire has-been.

Len's face drops

I can assure you that's where the similarity ends.

Doc Does she smoke a pipe?

Sally Only between overs.

Sound of lawn mower starting up. Shouts of "look out", off, screams, and a crash ending with a large bang

Doc What was that?

Freda Sounded like a hit and run lawn mower.

Ray comes running in. His white trousers have grass stains on them

Ray Doc, you'd better come quick. That young idiot Billy's started up lawn mower when Duncan had his fingers in blades.

Len Not his spinning finger! (*He moves to him*) Tell me it was his other hand.

Ray It's all right. He managed to pull his hand alway in time. He's just fainted.

Len He will be OK. Give him a glass of water.

Ray Young Billy also left the throttle on mower open so when it started up it flew across the pitch, chasing young Mary Thompson who's six months pregnant down to the third man boundary, shaved the vicar's dog and knocked Tommy Jeffries off his push bike, smashing his foot, before finally hitting a tree.

Len Is it smashed very bad?

Ray He'll need to go to hospital. I think it's his ligaments—he won't be playing any cricket today.

Len I meant the lawn mower—how badly broken is the mower?

All the men exit leaving the girls on their own

Freda Aren't you going to tell them?

Mary What and spoil all the fun.

Freda Don't they have newspapers up here?

Sally No, they still send all the important news tied to a pigeon's leg.

Jean comes in from the kitchen

Jean Oh, you're not reinforcements to help with the sandwiches?

Mary Afraid not.

Sally We are the opposition.

Jean's face drops

Jean It's all right. We do allow for the opposition to bring their wives. I'll just have to cut more sandwiches and you can come in and eat them after the men have finished. How does crab grab you?

Sally It doesn't I hope.

Jean Sorry?

Freda We are the opposition—it's us that's playing.

Jean But you're lasses.

Sally Yes we are, and there's something else—we're not from the West Indies.

Jean I didn't think you were—that coach is far too small to have come all the way from there—tell me does my husband know about you?

Mary He might do, I've got a terrible reputation.

Jean No, that you're here, I mean.

Freda There's a lot to choose from, which one's your husband?

Jean The captain.

Freda Oh, bad luck!

Jean I don't think he will be too happy playing a team of women.

Sally No, but he'll get used to it.

Doc comes in holding up Duncan with Billy walking behind them

Doc Sit down for a moment.

Jean What's wrong?

Duncan (*turning to Billy*) He tried to cut my bloody hand off, that's what's wrong!

Jean Which one?

Duncan Does it matter which one?

Jean It's just that they both look OK to me.

Duncan They are, but only because of my quick reactions.

Billy I'm sorry. How was I supposed to know you poked your fingers in the blades just as I started it up—anyway it would have stopped you biting your nails.

They all look at him

Just a joke!

Doc It's no joke, Billy. There's Tommy Jeffries on his way to hospital with a damaged foot because of you and that lawn mower.

Jean Good God, how did he get his foot in there?

Billy He tried to kick start it and slipped off!

They all look at him again

His foot wasn't in the mower, it just knocked him off his bike and twisted his ankle a bit.

Doc He'd have twisted your neck if he could have hopped faster.

Jean Where's Len?

Doc He's giving last rights to lawn mower.

Jean And Ray?

Billy He's all right. It only dragged him a few yards.

Jean What!

Billy Well he was holding the mower when it shot off.

Jean Is he all right?

Billy Ay, the stains should come out.

Jean Blood?

Billy No, grass.

Mary If you don't mind, we will go and have a practice in the nets with the rest of our team. That is if there's any of them out there still standing!

Doc Oh, yes. Your girls are quite all right.

Billy More than all right, most of them.

The girls go out

(*Watching them go*) Can you believe it—playing against a team of lasses. I can hardly wait.

Jean I shouldn't get too excited, you're only playing them at cricket.

Billy Who's worried about the cricket? I'm thinking about the showers afterwards. (*He rubs his hands together*)

Doc How are you feeling, Duncan?

Duncan I'm OK now, Doc. It was just the shock when it started.

Jean Take him to the kitchen and get him a cup of tea.

Billy I'll have one as well.

Jean You?

Billy Yes, it was a shock for me as well.

Jean Was it?

Billy I'll say. I didn't think that mower was ever going to go!

Doc, Duncan, and Billy go into the kitchen. Len enters, carrying the battered grass box from the lawn mower. Ray comes behind him carrying a buckled wheel

Jean (*looking at them*) Don't tell me—it's the antiques road show!

Len This is the only bit of mower not broken.

Ray (*holding up the wheel*) And Tommy's bike.

Len His wife's taken him to the hospital.

Jean How is he?

Len He's all right now, but his toes turned blue at one time and he couldn't feel them.

Jean Bruising.

Ray No, his bicycle clip had shot up his leg under his trousers and stopped the circulation.

Len It looks like that silly woman captain still wants to play.

Ray We might as well.

Len Yes, I'll go and talk to her. We will have to make a few changes so we get an even game mind. (*He turns to go out*) I'd best put this in the shed.

Ray Can you put this in there as well. (*He gives him the wheel*) Tommy might want it if he gets another bike.

Len I doubt it. He'll probably be too frightened to ever get back in the saddle. (*He takes the wheel and grass box*)

Len goes out

Jean (*turning to Ray*) Are you all right?

Ray Ay, of course.

Jean (*looking at his arm*) They said you were dragged along. Are you sure there's nothing broken.

Ray puts his arms round her

Ray Only my heart. When are you going to tell him about us?

Jean (*taking his hands away*) In time—when he's in a good mood.

Ray When was the last time he was in a good mood?

Jean When Yorkshire won the County Championship.

Ray That was years ago. I can't wait that long.

Jean We will just have to keep on seeing each other as we have been.

Ray I can't just keep seeing you when he goes out to bell ringing practice.

Jean Why not?

Ray It's not fair, that's why not—every time I hear a bell ring I get aroused.

Jean (*laughing*) Idiot!

Ray You can laugh, but it's not easy especially as I'm a fireman.

She laughs again

Why don't we run away?

Jean I don't think he'd be annoyed if you ran off with me—he'd be more upset if you took his cricket bat.

Ray Now who's being silly.

Jean I'm not, that bat's been on his lap more times than I have. He's always polishing it and the handle gets a new cover every year. I'm in the same coat he bought me ten years ago.

Ray Jean, there's something I want to tell you.

Pauline comes in

Jean (*seeing Pauline*) You'll need to soak that when you get home.

Ray What?

Jean To get the stain out.

He sees Pauline

Ray Oh yes.

Jean Hallo Pauline. Is the car all right?

Pauline Yes, it started first time.

Jean I hope you brought it straight up here.

Pauline No, I had a drive into town first.

Jean You'd better not had.

Pauline Of course I didn't, as if I dare.

Ray Doesn't he trust you in town.

Pauline He doesn't trust me anywhere.

Jean He's just careful. He doesn't like her wasting petrol that's all.

Pauline He makes Ebenezer Scrooge look like a spend thrift.

Jean Pauline!

Billy comes in followed by Doc and Duncan

Billy Hallo Pauline, you decided to come and watch me play then, have you?

Pauline How can I watch you play if you're twelfth man.

Ray looks at her

Ray How did you know he was twelfth man?

Pauline I–I was only joking—is he then?

Ray He was, but now that Tommy's injured, he'll play.

Pauline Tommy hurt?

Billy He fell off his push bike.

Ray He was knocked off it by your run-away lawn mower.

Billy Well, you was supposed to be holding it.

Ray looks at him, then goes out to the changing rooms

Duncan You never started it up when my hand was in it so that you'd get a game, did you?

Billy Duncan, it never entered my head—it's a good idea though.

Duncan If I thought you had I'd——

Doc Now boys, don't start that again.

Billy If I'm playing, I'd better go and warm up in the nets. Are you coming, Duncan?

Duncan No fear. If you cause so much devastation without even being warmed up, I'm not getting anywhere near you.

Billy Cheer up, Duncan. I hope you're not one of them that holds grudges.

Duncan After what you nearly did to me, I'm lucky to be able to hold anything at all.

Billy Not self-pity as well. I'm going to the nets. (*He starts to go out*)

Len comes in, followed by Mary

Billy and Len look at each other

I think he must be sucking the other half of Duncan's lemon.

Billy goes out

Len That boy's getting too big for his boots. (*He sees Pauline*) You're here are you. Is the car going yet.

Pauline That reminds me, I've left it running in car park for last twenty minutes.

Len You've done what!

Pauline Only joking, Dad. (*She throws him the keys*)

Len Kids these days think nothing of wasting money. (*To Pauline*) You're just like that young lad that works for me, what's his name?

Pauline Bob Cratchit.

Mary Look, can we just toss the coin so I can get back to my team.

Len Yes, of course. (*He looks in his pockets*) I don't seem to have any change on me.

Mary gives him a coin

Doc We are playing then?

Pauline I hope so or we will be eating crab paste sandwiches all week!

Len To make the sides fair, I've told their captain that they can have Billy on their side and we will play with ten men.

Mary There's really no need.

Len No, I insist, and to make it even fairer, I will come in at number ten for us.

Mary Look——

Len Please, (*he holds his hand up*) if it still looks a bit of a massacre, I will then proceed to bat left-handed—that should even things up a bit.

Doc Have you asked Billy if he will play for them?

Len No, I'll tell him in a moment.

Mary We don't want to play you if you've only got ten men.

Jack enters

Doc I tell you what, we will have the next man that turns up—someone's bound to.

Jean The curate comes up for a few sandwiches sometimes.

Len Yes, anyone will do.

Jack Our Leroy's outside, he'd have a game.

Len Who the heck's Leroy?

Jack He's my sister-in-law's boy.

Len A Yank?

Jack Ay.

Pauline (*excitedly*) From America?

Jack That's where most Yank's come from, ain't it?

Pauline (*moving towards the pavilion door*) I'm going to have a look at him.

Pauline exits

Jean (*running after her*) Pauline, you get yourself back here right now.

Jean exits

Len He can't play, he won't know the rules, and anyway they've got some disgusting habits, them Americans.

Doc We could teach him the rules as the game progresses, he'd soon pick it up.

Jack I doubt that, we've been trying to teach them to speak English for over a hundred years, but they don't seem to have got the hang of it as yet!

Doc It would be a challenge for us, Yorkshire's effort to further international sporting links between our two great countries.

Len What's he waffling on about, the lad's only going to stand on boundary and throw the ball back when it comes to him.

Doc So he is going to play then?

Len He'll have to, I suppose, but if he spits chewing-gum on my cricket square he's off.

Jack What about his mother?

Len She can spit as much as she likes.

Jack No—I mean she wants to watch the coin being tossed before the match starts.

Len Whatever for?

Jack Well it's probably the only bit of the game she'll understand.

Len All right—as long as she's quiet.

Jack goes outside

Mary Are we ever going to toss my coin, or are you just going to hold it all afternoon?

Len Ay, right.

Mary Heads.

Len What?

Mary I'll have heads.

Len You're supposed to call as the coin's in the air.

Mary Does it matter?

Len That is the proper way to do it.

Mary Give me strength!

Len Ready?

Alice, a large woman, comes in

Alice Howdy, everyone. How's all in merry little England?
Len (*turning*) Jack!—I thought you was keeping her qui . . . (*He looks at the woman*)
Alice Snuggle-bum! I'd recognize you anywhere.
Len (*in horror*) Alice! (*In fright, he drops the coin*)
Mary Heads!

Everyone looks at the coin, Len and Alice look at each other as——

—the CURTAIN *falls*

ACT II

The same. An hour and a half later

Jean is looking out of the window. Ray is sitting by the window doing the score book. Jack is walking backwards and forwards slowly. He is now wearing his cricket gear

Jean He's been out there umpiring all afternoon. Why doesn't he come back in and get someone else to do it like he normally does.

Ray He will have to soon. Fifty-two for seven. What a disaster. We'll be the laughing stock of Yorkshire.

Jean Beaten by a team of lasses. You'll all have to change your names and head south.

Ray Yes maybe—but they have got Billy playing for them. A fine young bowler is our Billy.

Jack Ay, but they haven't let him have a bowl yet—he's been stood on fine leg boundary picking his nose all afternoon!

Jean (*looking disgusted*) I hope he washes his hands before tea.

Ray They haven't needed to let him bowl, have they? Their opening bowler, Troutman, she's taken five wickets already.

Duncan walks out of the changing room. He wears a bandage on his head

Jack And the one she couldn't bowl out she knocked out—how's your ear, Duncan?

Duncan It feels like the head's come flying off a sledge-hammer and hit me in the lug 'ole, but apart from that I'm fine.

Jack You're not feeling sick or anything are you?

Duncan No, I'm fine. Why do you keep asking?

Jack No reason. (*He keeps walking up and down*)

Duncan The Doc's had a look at me ear and he says its OK. I've just got a bit of a Prince Charles flapper that's all.

Jean A what?

Ray His ear's swollen. (*He claps and cheers*) That's four more to Jim. (*He signals the umpire*) Its a good job he's playing.

Jack Are you insured, young Duncan?

Duncan Why?

Jack It just struck me that you're the kind of person that should be covered.

Duncan Covered!

Jack Ay, insurance.

Duncan Thank God for that. I thought you meant dirt.

Jack You just seem very accident prone to me. (*He continues to walk up and down*)

Ray Do you have to keep walking about. It's very off putting when you're trying to score.

Duncan That's what all the girls tell him.

Jack I can't help it—it's the job.

Jean What?

Ray He's been an undertaker for so long, funeral pace is the only speed he can move at.

Jack And I always walk with me right shoulder slightly stooped.

Jean Arthritis, I suppose.

Jack No it's to stop the coffin sliding off.

Pauline comes in from outside

Pauline Where's Leroy?

Duncan If you mean the Yank, he's outside—learning to run in his cricket pads.

Pauline Of course I mean the American, who else would I be talking about?

Duncan No-one in Yorkshire, not with a name like Leroy, that's for sure.

Pauline Oh, he's such a hunk, isn't he!

Duncan He don't do a lot for me.

Jean Why are you still here? You don't normally stay.

Pauline I've got nothing else to do.

Jean You never have, but you don't stay and watch cricket.

Duncan Maybe it's not the cricket she's watching!

Jean Still it will be nice to have someone to help with the teas.

Pauline's face drops

Your father's been out umpiring all afternoon. He'll be parched when he comes in.

Duncan I've never seen him so keen to get the coat on.

Ray Yes, it was as soon as those Yanks walked in, Len won the toss, shouted we'll bat, grabbed the umpire's coat and ran out.

Pauline He even forgot to put the coin in his pocket.

Duncan It wasn't his coin.

Pauline That's never stopped him before.

Ray It must have been the Yanks putting him off.

Jean Ay—he never did have a lot of time for foreigners

Clapping from outside

Ray Good shot, Jim, that's four more (*He acknowledges the umpires signal*) Look out there, poor old Leroy's going to have a job going for any quick singles in those trousers.

All look out of the window

Duncan They look a bit tight around middle stump—I'll say that.

Pauline He can't help it, it's Tommy Jeffries' kit.

Jack But it doesn't fit.

Pauline Of course it doesn't, Leroy's three times bigger than Tommy.
Duncan I wonder if he's wearing a box?
Pauline No he's not.
Jean How do you know!
Pauline Those trousers are so tight he can only just do the zip up.
Jack I'll get him a strap-on box. Then he can wear it on the outside (*He walks to the changing room*) We don't want him getting hit and spoiling his holiday on the first day.

He exits

Pauline I did ask if he was wearing anything for protection.
Duncan What did he say?
Pauline He said "You English girls don't hang about, do you."
Jean You're getting too clever by half, my girl.

Jack comes out of the changing rooms. He is carrying a strap-on box

Jack Here give him this. (*He holds up the box*)
Pauline What is it? A sling shot? (*She takes the box*)
Jean (*grabbing it from her*) Put it down, you don't know where it's been! (*She throws it on the table*)
Duncan She's the only one that doesn't then.
Jean I'll find you something to do in the kitchen to keep your mind occupied.

They exit to the kitchen

Jack You take it to him.
Duncan All right. (*He takes the box*)

Duncan exits

A big shout of "How's that" off

Ray He'll have to hurry—Doc's just gone for a second run and didn't make it. Leroy's in, go and get him out.
Jack Don't start saying things like that to him he'll only get more confused.
Ray (*pointing out of the window*) He hasn't even got a bat!
Jack I'll get him one. (*He walks to the changing rooms*) Yanks. Makes you wonder how they ever found their way to the moon and back.

He goes into the changing room

Ray (*to himself*) At least Len will have to come in now. Him and Jim may be able to get some runs.

Jack enters with bat

Jack I tried to show him how to use one of these earlier, but the only thing he hit was his toe!
Ray You'd better get it to him anyway, he's on his way out, without one.

Jack goes out, Duncan enters

Ray Is he strapped in?
Duncan Just about. (*He crosses to Ray*) I gave him the box and said put it on, you don't want to get hit with the ball like I did.
Ray So, did he put it on?
Duncan Yeah, sort of—he started strapping it to his ear.
Ray Oh no!
Duncan I showed him where to put it and he agreed it made more sense.

Doc enters

Doc What does that American boy look like! Who's idea was it to let him play?
Ray Yours!
Doc Oh—and a very good one it was too—it's about time these Americans learnt how to play a civilized game. How's your head, Duncan?
Duncan Throbbing!
Doc Good! You'll remember to take it out the way next time. (*He starts to take his pads off*)
Ray He's just got to the middle.

The girls are heard off, whistling and shouting

Freda (*off*) Look girls, we've got ourselves a ballet dancer!
Sally (*off*) I hope that's not all hanky in them trousers!

Len comes in

Len Do you hear that? Clear intimidation of one of our players. Mind you, he does look like a knock-kneed stork.
Ray It's all kit we had. Anyway, he won't be in long. Doc, can you do the score book?
Doc Yes, indeed.
Ray They crossed over so Leroy won't have to face yet.

Doc sits at the window

Ray exits to the kitchen

Duncan By the way, Leroy's mum wanted a word with you.
Len (*agitated*) What about?
Duncan She wouldn't tell me but it must have been important. She was half-way out to the wicket to see you when I stopped her.
Len Yes, well—she probably wanted my autograph. You know what these Yanks are like.
Duncan I'm going for a walk. I'll tell her you're here if I see her. (*He moves to the pavilion door*)
Len No!

Duncan turns

I mean I've got all me work cut out trying to win us the game—I don't want her in here spoiling me concentration before I go in to bat.
Duncan What will I tell her?

Len Tell her anything you like, but don't let her near me.
Duncan Your wife's right.
Len What about?
Duncan You don't like foreigners, do you?

Duncan goes out

Len picks up a set of pads and puts one leg on the chair putting them on

Len Nice little knock you had there, Doc. I'm glad to see that someone as well as me in club can face fast bowling.
Doc (*looking out of the window*) I just kept an end up really. Jim got most of the runs. (*Shouting*) Good shot, James.

Len looks out of the window

Len He only got a single.
Doc Yes, but it was from the last ball of the over, so Leroy doesn't have to face Freda Troutman.

Len starts putting on the other pad

Alice creeps in the doorway

She goes up to Len and grabs him round the waist. In shock, Len throws the pad away

Alice How's my Snuggle bum, then?
Len Madam, do you mind. (*He backs off*)
Alice You know I don't mind, not with you, Snuggle bum.

Jean comes in from the kitchen

Jean What's all the noise about?
Len It's all right, dear—just picking up my pad.
Jean Who's Snuggle bum?
Len What?
Jean Snuggle bum?
Len Ah ... a ... a ... it's this lady's cat ... she's lost it.
Jean Oh dear, what a shame. After bringing it all the way from America as well.
Len No—no, she found it—it's a stray she picked up today.
Jean Yes—she seems very good at doing that.

Jean turns and goes back to the kitchen

Len Can't you see. You're annoying my wife.
Alice Oh, Snuggle bum's upset with Alice.
Len Look, I've told you before. I'm not the person your looking for—do I look like a Snuggle bum?
Alice Not now—you're more of a saggy bum now. But twenty-five years ago you were a Snuggle bum and I was your Alice.

Len is slowly backing away from Alice who is moving towards him. Doc can't keep his eyes off them

We were young and foolish; two ships that met briefly in the night, before fate forced them to take separate courses. Their paths never to cross again until today.

Len I tell you, you've got the wrong ship.

Alice I'd recognize you anywhere. Same boyish good looks, same sparkling eyes and that same cheeky smile you always had—maybe not the same teeth, but I still recognize the smile.

Doc watches

Len (*backed up against the wall*) Look!

Alice You were so strong—so passionate—so demanding—so—so . . .

Doc Drunk?

Alice Yes.

Len Not so loud please. (*He points to Doc*)

Alice looks at him

Doc Don't mind me—I'm a doctor.

Alice If you don't know me, why did you shout my name when I came in?

Len I didn't!

Alice You did! I shouted Snuggle bum and you answered Alice.

Len (*moving away from her*) I did? No—no, what it was is when you came in, me and the other team's captain had just tossed a coin to see who would field first and I lost so I shouted "Alas!"

Doc (*shaking his head*) Amazing!

Len That's what you must have got confused with.

Doc It's incredible what the brain can come up with when cornered.

Alice We'll soon settle this. Roll up your sleeve!

Doc Arm wrestling?

Alice My man has a tattoo here (*she pats her arm*)—a sign of undying love he said.

Doc Till he sobered up, then it became an unloving dye!

Len You're not helping, Doc.

Duncan comes in from outside

Duncan Doc, as you're scoring, would you please acknowledge the umpire's signal of a leg-bye—he's been hopping on one leg so long, he's fallen over!

Doc Sorry. (*He turns to the window and puts his hand up*)

Duncan I see your fan club's caught up with you then, Skip.

Duncan turns and exits

Alice That young man told me I couldn't see you because you were on the treatment table.

Len Well, I was under the doctor earlier.

Doc That leg-bye means Leroy's got to face his first ball.

Len Oh, no! Where's me gloves?

Alice It's not cold out there.

Len I'm going to have to bat in a moment. (*He picks up his gloves*)

Pauline runs in from the kitchen

Pauline It's Leroy. It's his turn to bat, I'm going to watch.

Pauline runs outside. Ray comes in from the kitchen

Ray Leroy's going to face his first ball.

Len walks away not liking all the attention Leroy's getting

Jean walks in from the kitchen

Jean Leroy's facing.
Len Well, I would never have guessed!

Jean walks away from him to join the rest looking out of the window. Len goes through a few practice shots, not interested

Alice Why's that woman walking away? Doesn't she want to see my Leroy play?
Doc Madam, that's the bowler going back to her run up.
Ray She's on her way now!
Pauline (*off*) Go on, Leroy, you can do it!
Ray Oh no, he's took one hand off the bat to wave.
Doc She'll kill him!

Len smiles to himself, then there is the sound of a ball being hit hard off

Ray No! He's hit it back over the bowler's head—it's got to be a six.

Len frowns

Doc Look, he's thrown his bat down and run off around the square-leg umpire—what's he doing?
Ray Oh no—he thinks he's playing baseball! He's running around the outside of the pitch.
Jean He's been given out anyway.

Len smiles to himself

Len Caught on the boundary, I suppose.
Jean No, the ball went for a six, but when he threw down his bat he knocked his wickets over.

They all move away from the window

I'd better get tea.
Len Hang on, I've got to bat yet!
Jean Then I'll put the kettle on, it takes five minutes to boil.

Jean goes out to the kitchen. Jack and Pauline come in from outside

Jack The young fool—I told him to run from end to end, not run all round ground like a demented whippet.
Pauline He did all right, you shouldn't have shouted at him.
Alice Where's my Leroy?
Jack He went off in a bit of a huff.

Pauline I'm not surprised after what you called him.

Jack He wouldn't have understood what I was saying.

Pauline Jack—I think your word "pillock" is pretty universal!

Alice It's not my Leroy's fault, he hit the ball so far he thought it was a home run—and instinct took over.

Pauline He tried his best.

Len Yes he did, but it wasn't good enough. (*He puts his cap on*) Cometh the hour, cometh the man.

Len swaggers out the door to bat

Jack Didn't he get that saying from Churchill?

Pauline I don't know about that, but he got the walk from John Wayne!

Alice I'd recognize that walk anywhere.

Pauline I'm going to find Leroy.

Jack When you do, tell him from me he done all right.

Pauline He'll appreciate that.

Jack For a Yank that is.

Pauline goes out

Alice (*going to Jack*) Did you see the way that man in the dirty white raincoat kept making rude gestures at Leroy?

Jack He's an umpire.

Alice Well, Mr Umpire wants to watch his manners, he stuck his finger up at my Leroy. (*She holds her middle finger up*)

Doc In cricket when the umpire sticks his finger up at you it means your out!

Alice Oh ... Oh well ... I wouldn't like to tell you what it means in America. (*She puts her finger down*)

Shout of "How's that" off

Doc Oh no—he's out first ball again.

Jack Not the skipper?

Doc Afraid so.

The door flies open and Len storms in

Len (*annoyed*) The great stupid pillock! No-one can bat out there with an idiot of an umpire like that. (*He throws his bat down*) That ball was missing leg stump by six inches and he stands there with his finger stuck up in the air.

Alice He must stop that, he's annoying everybody.

Len You can shut up, an' all! (*He throws his gloves down*)

Alice Same flaring nostrils.

Len Ahhhhhh! (*He jumps up and down on his bat*)

Jean comes in from the kitchen

Jean You're back are you?

Len Of course I'm back—what do you think it is, a cardboard cut out.

Jean The kettle hasn't even boiled yet.

She goes back into the kitchen. Alice follows her

Doc That's it then. All out for seventy. Looks like an early tea.

Len No, it's not.

Doc I don't understand, if we are all out ...

Len That's just it. We're not all out.

Ray What do you mean?

Len Jack, go and get Duncan.

Jack exits outside

Ray You can't expect him to go back in!

Len Why not? He only retired hurt, he wasn't out.

Doc But he's had a crack on the ear.

Len Well, he's got another one, hasn't he?

Doc As a doctor, I must advise against it. He's got a bit of double vision—he'll be seeing two balls.

Len Good, then he might be able to hit one of them this time.

Duncan comes in from outside

Duncan You wanted me, Skip.

Len (*standing up*) Ay, yes Duncan, I do. (*He puts his arm around his shoulders*) I wouldn't ask this if I didn't think you were the right man for the job.

Duncan I know what you want, Skip—and you can rely on me.

Len turns and looks at everyone else and smiles

Len (*to Duncan*) Spoken like a true Yorkshireman.

Duncan I'll do the job as best I can.

Doc I'd advise against it, Duncan.

Duncan No, Doc—I don't mind doing the washing-up after tea. Someone's got to do it.

Len I'm not talking about washing-up! I'm talking about going back out to bat.

Duncan (*shocked*) B—Back out there! With that mad woman throwing the ball at me head like it were a coconut shy.

Len We need more runs, Duncan—I don't—we don't want to get beat by a load of lasses. I can't order you to go—but you're the only one that can do it for team.

Duncan (*thinking*) All right, I'll do it.

Len Good man. (*He pats him on the back*)

Duncan But only if I can wear a helmet.

Len A helmet! Where can I get a cricket helmet from? We've never needed one before.

Ray Billy came on his motorbike—his crash helmet is in the changing room.

Len That will do, go and get it.

Ray goes out to the changing rooms as Jack comes in from outside

Len Jack, go and tell their captain that our last batsman is coming out.
Jack I've always wanted to be a messenger boy.

Jack turns and goes outside as Ray comes back in with the crash helmet

Doc Do you think this is a good idea, Duncan. I don't like you going back out there, not after the bang on the head you took before.
Len He's all right, look. (*He turns to Duncan and holds up two fingers*) How many fingers, Duncan?
Duncan Who?
Len There you are, two—he's as right as rain.

Len takes the helmet from Ray and pushes it on Duncan's head. Duncan cries out because of his ear. Len puts Duncan's pads and bat into his arms

Just get out there and try to let Jim have the bowling.

Duncan tries to say something

Ray He's trying to say something.

Len opens the visor

Duncan I've just thought—she's on a hat-trick.
Len Don't worry, it won't be as good as yours.

Len pushes the visor down and turns Duncan to the door

  Duncan exits

Len turns back into the room. Everyone is looking at him

That's what I like to see. Someone with a bit of backbone in the team.

  Len goes out to the kitchen

Ray walks over to the scoring table and sits with Doc

CURTAIN

SCENE 2

The same. After tea the same day

Sally, Mary and Freda are sitting talking to each other. There are empty plates and cups on the table

Sally Burp!
Mary Sally!
Sally Sorry—it's the cucumber in the sandwiches.
Freda I'm not surprised—you did eat two platefuls of them.
Sally I was hungry—anyway no-one else wanted them.
Freda Nobody else was brave enough to put their hands in to get one, you mean.
Mary I felt sorry for their last batsman.
Freda You mean the one that came back in after I'd knocked him out.

Sally picks up the last piece of celery

Sally He was wearing a crash helmet the second time. When Freda ran up to bowl at him, his knees were knocking like a pair of castanets. (*She bites into the celery*) Least I think it was his knees, it was hard to say. He was twitching like a water diviner's twig in a submarine.

Mary When they put that helmet on him, it made his ear swell up even more. So after he came back in, it took them ten minutes to get it off again!

Freda By which time, you'd pushed two plates of sandwiches down your throat and drunk his tea!

Sally It was getting cold!

Freda (*turning to Mary*) When are you going to tell them the truth?

Mary Not just yet—we'll bat a bit first.

Sally I want to see their captain's face when they find out.

Freda I wonder why they haven't caught on?

Sally Nothing catches on in Yorkshire, most of them still wear bell bottom trousers.

Len comes in followed by Doc, Duncan and Jack. Duncan wears an even bigger bandage on his ear

Len Right, ladies, that's the pitch rolled for the start of your innings.

Jack sits down on the chair. Freda goes to him and looks

Freda Did he pull the roller on his own? He looks ill.

Len Of course he didn't. It was a team effort under my guidance of course.

Jack He sits on the roller to give it extra weight.

Len I'm opening the bowling—you don't expect me to push roller as well.

Freda (*still looking at Jack*) He doesn't look very well.

Doc He's an undertaker. It's bad for business to look too healthy.

Jack I keep me self dusted down with French chalk. You have to look as though you're at death's door so people think you know what you're doing when you put their relatives in ground.

Freda runs her finger down Jack's face, looks at it then looks at the other girls

(*To Len*) You've done something to your hair as well.

Len No, I haven't!

Freda It's all swept back.

Doc It was probably due to the speed we were pushing the roller.

Freda rubs Len's head and looks at her hand

Freda No!—he's put Brylcreem on it.

Sally Brylcreem! I thought that stuff went out with the spitfire.

Len It's only to keep my hair in place while I'm bowling.

Doc It's not strictly playing to the rules, Skipper.

Len It's to stop it falling in my eyes.

Mary You wouldn't use it to rub on the ball to get some extra shine on it when you're bowling, would you?

Everyone looks at him

Len No, of course I wouldn't. (*He sees everyone is still looking at him*) It's to keep the hair out of my bloody eyes, so I can see what I'm doing.

Freda You didn't wear anything when you were batting.

Len No, that's why I was out first ball—now are we going to play cricket or admire my hair-style all the rest of the afternoon?

Mary My girls are ready.

Doc You'll have to wash your hair, Skipper. I can't go out there to play knowing you've got something on your head that's not natural and could help us win the game.

Len looks at Doc

Len All right—all right, I'll wash it in the sink in the changing rooms. Will that be all right?

Doc I think it will be best.

Mary Well—we will see you after you've had your hair done then, Skipper.

Len glares at them as they move to the pavilion door

Mary and Sally exit

Freda (*moving to Len*) Don't stay under that dryer too long, dear, it gives you a terrible headache!

She goes out laughing

Len starts barking out the orders

Len Where's Ray? He knows we've got to go and do our warm up exercises before we start fielding.

Duncan He's helping your wife with the washing-up.

Len I'm beginning to wonder about him.

Doc What do you mean?

Len He sets such a bad example to the rest of the team. What would they say if they went into the kitchen and saw him up to his elbows in soap suds?

Duncan Shall I go and get him?

Len No, leave him, but if he pulls a muscle it will be his own fault. Come on. (*He goes to the pavilion door*)

Doc Aren't you forgetting something?

Len What?

Doc Your hair.

Len Oh, ay. You lot go on, I'll be there in two ticks.

They all go outside. Len goes to the changing rooms. After he's gone, Ray enters from the kitchen. He is wearing a pinny and rubber gloves with a tea towel tucked in the waist. He goes to the table and starts clearing up plates. Jean enters from the kitchen with a tray

Jean You don't want to let Len see you dressed like that.

Ray Do you think he'll have me coming in two mornings a week to do the silver?

Jean More like shot at dawn with a tea towel for a blind fold for impersonating the enemy.

Ray I don't know how you put up with him.

Jean You get used to him. It takes some believing, I know, but he was quite the little gentleman when I first met him.

Ray What went wrong?

Jean He woke up. (*She puts the plates on the tray*)

Ray Jean, you know I was trying to tell you something earlier on, but someone came in?

Jean Yes.

Ray This may be the only chance I'll get—before I have to field that is.

Jean Oh!

Ray I'm moving.

Jean What, house?

Ray I suppose so, yes.

Jean I know, you've bought one of them new flats on the edge of the village. They'd be ideal as you're on your own.

Ray No—I'm moving from Yorkshire.

Jean (*trying not to show that she is upset*) Where are you moving to? Far is it? (*She continues to pick up plates*)

Ray London.

Jean (*stopping*) That far? (*She turns and moves towards the kitchen*) Still, I've heard it's nice there, what with the pollution and pigeon droppings. You should have the time of your life.

Ray goes to her, grabs her arm and turns her around to him

Ray Jean!

Jean Ray—why? (*Crying*) If you go, what will I do?

Ray takes the tray puts it on the floor, then gives her the tea towel to dry her eyes

You're the only thing that keeps me sane in this place. (*She blows her nose in the towel*) Have you been transferred by the fire brigade?

Ray Sort of. (*He takes off the gloves*)

Jean Why?

Ray Well, you know how it is. You meet a better class of fire in London!

Jean Please don't joke.

Ray I'm sorry. They're not transferring me, I asked for one actually.

Jean (*looking at him*) Oh—I see.

Ray Not only did they grant me a transfer, they gave me promotion as well.

Jean Congratulations. I'm so happy for you. (*She starts crying again*)

Ray Why don't you come with me?

She looks at him

Jean To London?

Ray Why not?

Jean I couldn't—all those people—all the noise and dirt.

Ray The shops—the theatre—you'd love it!

Jean But I feel closed in if four people get in the car with me. I couldn't live like they do down there.

Ray So you won't come with me?

Jean Oh, Ray. (*She puts her hand to his face*)

Ray I want you to. Nothing would give me greater pleasure.

Jean What about Pauline?

Ray I hadn't thought of asking her!

Jean Fool—I can't leave her, she needs her mum.

Ray So do I.

Jean What would she think of me.

Ray Pauline's not a little girl any more, the only person who thinks she is, is your husband. I tell you Pauline won't spend all her life in Yorkshire.

Jean When are you going?

Ray Next week. I didn't think there was much point hanging around.

Jean No, I suppose there isn't.

Ray So what's it to be.

Jean I can't think straight, my head's going round.

Ray Come on, pack a bag and let's go chase a rainbow.

Jean I don't need to pack.

Ray What?

Jean Len and me are supposed to be going away for a few days next week. I've got all my stuff in a separate case so I don't crease his shirts.

Ray Good, then we'll go tonight.

Jean What!—now I know you're mad.

Billy comes in from outside

Jean moves away from Ray

Hello Billy, enjoying the game?

Billy If you can call standing on the boundary all afternoon enjoyment, I am—I didn't get a bowl and from how them lasses are hitting the ball in the nets, I won't be getting a bat neither.

Ray There's something very peculiar about this team.

Billy You can say that again. Have you seen Pauline?

Jean Yes, her and Leroy took their teas out to have a little picnic.

Billy A little picnic! (*Upset, he goes to the door and turns*) I ask you what has this Leroy got that I haven't?

Ray An American passport.

Billy shrugs his shoulders and walks out

Ray Well what's your answer?

Jean takes a key from her pocket and gives it him

Jean Make sure you get the blue case. I don't want to be wearing Len's off-the-peg suits in the capital.

He takes the key

Ray Don't worry, you can get away with anything in London. I'll go out the back way. (*He starts to go through the kitchen door*)
Jean Ray! ˜
Ray What?
Jean This isn't London.
Ray Sorry?
Jean You'd better take the pinny off.
Ray Oh, ay. (*He quickly takes the pinny off*) See you in about fifteen minutes

He goes out

Jean The fool's supposed to be fielding. (*She picks up the pinny and gloves, and puts them on the tray*)

She exits to the kitchen carrying the tray

Len enters from the changing room wiping his hair

He sees no-one is about and goes over to the umpire's coat on the back of the chair. He takes the ball from the pocket and takes it to the table. He gets a bottle of shampoo from his pocket, takes the lid off and pours some on the shiny side of the ball. He rubs it with the towel.

Len So they won't let me use Brylcreem will they—let's see what a drop of shampoo does for the ball.

A noise from off stage, Len quickly puts the ball back in the umpire's coat pocket, sees the shampoo still on the table. He runs back and puts it upside down in his pocket

Doc comes in from outside

Doc I wanted a quick word with you, Skipper.
Len Oh yes, what about? (*He sees the top of the shampoo bottle on the table and feels shampoo running down his leg*)
Doc It's about that American woman.
Len What about her? (*He moves his leg*)
Doc Is she the one on your arm?
Len (*turning to him*) Shhhh! (*He turns back because Doc can see the shampoo*) I thought you doctors were supposed to be discreet about your patients' private lives.
Doc We are.
Len Then why are you coming in here—shouting about— (*he realizes he is shouting and lowers his voice*) shouting about my tattoo?
Doc I wasn't shouting and anyway, I'm not your doctor.
Len It doesn't matter, you're all supposed to have taken the hypocritical oath or something, haven't you?
Doc Why are you hopping about?
Len I'm just a bit nervous about bowling that's all.
Doc It's nothing to get yourself in a lather about.

Len No, your probably right, Doc, but I don't seem to be able to help it at the moment.

He walks out stiff legged to the changing rooms

Doc stands watching him

Mary comes in from outside

Mary It looks like I'm umpiring for a while.
Doc Oh well, somebody's got to—and I've no doubt you're better qualified than most of us.
Mary (*looking at him*) Maybe. (*She puts the umpire's coat on and takes the ball out. She looks at it, puts it to her nose and smells it*) It smells of soap. (*She lets Doc smell it*)
Doc Smells more like suntan oil. (*He looks at the shampoo top*)
Mary (*sniffing again*) No, definitely soap of some sort. Who needs suntan oil the weather we've been having?
Doc (*holding the shampoo top*) You will be later—about Christmas time.

She looks at him

Mary Not much chance of catching a tan in December.
Doc No—not in this country anyway, but you look like a team that doesn't mind a spot of travelling for a game of cricket.
Mary Maybe.
Doc Anyway, cricket seems to be your forte.
Mary You know, don't you?
Doc Yes, I worked in London before I moved to Tetford.
Mary Bad luck—but someone's got to do the missionary work up here.
Doc I don't mind, I love the place. But before I went in to tea I phoned a friend of mine back in London who's well in with the cricket scene.
Mary Why haven't you told the others?
Doc (*looking at the shampoo top in his hand*) Well, let's just say that some of us deserve to be taken for a ride.

Len comes back with a new pair of trousers

Len Oh, I see you've got the match ball.
Mary Yes. (*She looks at Doc and puts it back in the pocket*)
Doc I see you've changed your trousers as well as washing your hair.
Mary He must be going out somewhere special.
Len These are me bowling trousers.
Doc There's no red mark on the leg where the ball's supposed to be polished—or don't you need to?
Len These are me brand new bowling trousers, unused until today.
Mary Yes.

They both look at him

Len Anyway, there's no law about a man changing his trousers, is there?
Mary (*walking to the door*) No, not that I know of unless of course he does it in the high street—we will start the innings in five minutes, shall we?

She goes out

Len Right!

Doc There's nothing you want to tell me is there, Skipper. No little secret I could help you unburden.

Len Oh . . . no, Doc . . . I've never felt less unburdened.

Doc Good, because I've got a lot of respect for you, Skipper. When I first met you, I thought there's a man to respect—a bowler who stands head and shoulders above everyone else. (*He throws the bottle cap to Len who catches it*)

Len What's this?

Doc (*hard*) It's a cap for your Head and Shoulders.

They look at each other

Doc turns and goes out

Len looks at the top in his hand

Len You'd think I wasn't doing it for the team.

He throws the top into the corner

Alice comes in

What do you want? Can't you leave me alone—if you're still looking for this man Snuggle bum?

Alice No—no, I'm not looking anymore.

Jean opens the kitchen door to listen. The audience sees her but Len and Alice don't

Alice I'd like a few words with you if I could—if it's not taking up too much of your precious time.

Len As a matter of fact I've got to open the bowling in five minutes.

Alice That's OK because what I've got to say to you will only take two!

Len Anything to help clear up the misunderstanding.

Alice Yes, well I'm afraid that's my fault.

Len (*surprised*) It is . . . ! I mean, it is?

Alice Yes, you see, you couldn't have been the man I met twenty-five years ago.

Len That's what I've been telling you. (*He turns from her*)

Alice The young man I knew was kind, warm and understanding. You see, you may think that I'd come back here to make trouble for this man, but that's not so. What happened all those years ago is history in the past, and I've learnt today that it's not always a good idea to go back and play around with what's gone by.

Len (*a bit hurt*) Yes—well—as long as someone's learnt their lesson.

Alice Oh yes, yes I have and I can't tell you how glad I am that I've been able to discount you from my enquiries—and I won't have to tell Leroy that the jumped up, arrogant pig-headed son of a bitch of a cricket captain is his pa!

Len is totally shocked—he stands open mouthed. Alice moves slowly to the door

We all make mistakes when we're young—but I think I've just stopped myself making an even bigger one this afternoon. (*She looks around*) For the rest of my vacation, I'm going to have a great time in England.

Pauline comes in

Pauline Dad, you've got to come and see Leroy.

She gets no response

Dad!
Len What?
Pauline You've got to see Leroy, he wants to know where he stands.
Len (*urgently*) What do you mean where he stands?
Pauline When he's fielding—you've got to tell him where to stand.
Len Oh, yes. I'll be out in a moment.

Pauline exits

Alice looks at her

Alice She's a lovely girl—she must take after her ma—if you don't change, you'll lose her.
Len What do you mean?
Alice Your wife's a nice lady as well—she must have tremendous self control.
Len What are you going on about?
Alice (*looking at her watch*) I'd like to tell you, but it would take one heck of a lot longer than the two minutes you've got left.

Alice goes out. Jean goes back into the kitchen and shuts the kitchen door

Len thinks hard to himself for a long time. He seems to make up his mind about something and walks to the kitchen door

Duncan comes in from outside

Duncan There you are, Skip—we're all waiting on you to bowl.
Len Oh yes—right oh, Duncan.
Duncan We can't find Ray so I asked Billy if he would field for us—he moaned like a farmer with a toothache at first, but he said he would. He's a good lad really, is Billy.
Len (*not listening*) What's that Duncan?
Duncan I said Billy, he's a good lad.
Len (*looking at him*) Yes—yes he is, isn't he? And a damn fine bowler. (*He pats Duncan on the shoulder*) Well done, Duncan, you've taken a weight off me mind.
Duncan I only asked if he'd field for a bit.
Len Quick thinking—that's what makes leaders, (*he moves back to him*) and I haven't thanked you for putting on those extra twenty runs before tea— well done!

Len goes out leaving Duncan open mouthed

Duncan Bloody hell! I've done something right.

He follows Len out—after they've gone Jean comes out from the kitchen. She walks around thinking to herself

Jean A son. He's always wanted a boy. (*She walks around again*)

Freda and Sally come in from outside

Freda Do you mind if we sit by the window to do the score book? The clouds are starting to gather out there.
Jean Yes, of course.

They go to the table by the window and both sit down

Freda I must say, that was a very nice tea you put on.
Sally Yes it was—it's a pity I'm on a diet though.
Jean (*uncertain*) Oh—I see, a diet.
Freda She's only having you on—she eats like a sumo wrestler really.
Sally You're so kind—I'm really touched!
Freda I could have told you that, dear. (*She looks out of the window*) Hang on, that big ox of a captain's about to bowl.

Sally elbows her

I mean, your husband's about to bowl the first ball.
Jean (*not interested*) Oh.

A loud bang on the pavilion roof makes Jean jump

What was that?

Clapping is heard from outside

Sally That was the ball hitting the roof. Our opening batswoman just hit a six.
Jean Oh dear—he won't like that very much.
Sally He seems to be smiling.
Jean It'll be indigestion. He's forgotten his Rennies again.
Freda It must be a chronic case then—he's laughing now.
Jean No. (*She runs to the window*) Your batsman must have hurt herself.
Sally She's all right—they're both laughing.
Jean Well, I never.
Freda Your husband appears to have ripped his trousers.
Sally Oh yes, how embarrassing. That will be draughty for him.
Freda Looks like you got yourself a sewing job later.
Jean Not me, our Pauline's the seamstress of the family.
Sally Really?
Jean Oh yes—give her the material and she'll run you up anything you like, a real art it is.
Freda We'll be looking for——

Sally elbows her again

Jean What?

Sally She was just saying we will be looking for a quick victory so we can get down the pub.

Jean You don't have to worry about going too far for that, we've got a lovely club-house out the back.

Sally Do they do food?

Jean Yes, I do.

Sally Not crab paste sandwiches, is it?

Jean No, in the evening it's pie and mushy peas but I can't cook it tonight.

Sally Why not—got a heavy date, have we?

Jean No of course I haven't. Who's told you that?

Sally Just a joke.

Clapping from outside

Freda Great shot—that's four more. (*To Jean*) What's that behind them trees.

Jean (*looking*) That's the canal—why?

Freda That's where the ball's gone.

Jean There's more cricket balls in that canal than there ever was fish came out of it.

Sally They've gone to look for it.

Jean They won't find it, they never do.

Freda It doesn't matter, it's started to rain—they're coming in.

Jean I'd best put the kettle on.

She goes to the kitchen. Len comes in with his jumper tied around his waist, followed by Billy, Duncan and Mary

Len Duncan, tell the rest of them to go to the club-house.

Duncan Right.

Len Tell them the bar will be open in two minutes—(*he turns to Mary*)—that's if you haven't any objections.

Mary Me? No—five minutes of rain like this and it will be too wet to play anyway.

Len Good. (*He gives Duncan the keys*)

Duncan But it's only five o'clock.

Len So?

Duncan It's too early. You've never opened the bar early before.

Len Then it's about time I started, now off with you.

Duncan goes outside closely followed by an eager Mary, Freda and Sally

Pauline comes in

Pauline Dad, Leroy doesn't know what to do, he's all wet.

Billy Poor Leroy, don't they get rain in America then?

Pauline Of course they do, sometimes a lot more than we get here.

Billy That must explain why they've got bigger drips.

Pauline pokes her tongue out at him

Len Billy, why don't you go and buy our American cousins a drink.
Billy *What!*
Len Show them how friendly us Yorkshire folk can be.
Billy (*looking at Pauline*) I thought someone else was already doing that.
Len (*taking his wallet from his pocket*) Here, I'll get the first round. (*He gives Billy a ten pound note*) If it's not enough, tell whoever's behind the bar, I'll square up later.
Billy (*taking it slowly*) Are you all right, Skip? I didn't think you liked foreigners?
Len We've all got to live together—give everyone pie and mushy peas if they want as well.
Pauline You know that means a lot more work for Mum.
Len No, it won't. I'm going to have a shower then I'm going to cook it myself.
Pauline You! You don't even know where the kitchen is.

The pavilion door opens Jack is standing there soaking wet, holding the cricket ball

Jack I'd like to thank everyone for helping me get cricket ball from canal. (*He throws the ball on the floor*)
Len You found it!
Billy First time anyone's got the ball out of there! How did you do it?
Jack When I got to the bank there was soap suds on the top of water, so I put me hand in and pulled ball out first time—I'm going for a shower.
Billy But the skipper's given us a tenner to get a drink.
Jack Ah, then perhaps I'll have a pint first then get a shower.

Everyone, except Len, troops towards the door

Len I'd like a word with you, Pauline.
Pauline (*turning*) I've done nothing wrong.

Billy and Jack exit. Jean comes and listens at the kitchen door

Len I know that. It's me that's done wrong. Sit down, will you, I want a word.
Pauline What about? (*She comes back and sits at the table*)
Len Well—it's a bit awkward for me.
Pauline Look, if it's the birds and the bees, we did it in the last year at school.
Len No, it's not that.
Pauline Then what—I was talking to Leroy.
Len You like him, don't you?
Pauline Not really—he talks about himself all the time.
Len But you're always with him.
Pauline Oh that—it's only to make Billy jealous.
Len Yes—he's a nice lad Billy.
Pauline (*confused*) Are we talking about the same Billy that you threatened to cripple if he walked up our garden path again?

Len We all do and say stupid things. It's just that it take some of us most our lives to see it, that's all.

Pauline goes to him

Pauline Dad, what's wrong?
Len I've been silly, Pauline—an old fool, can you find it in your heart to forgive me?

She puts her arms around him

Pauline Oh, Dad, it's not me you've got to say this to—it's Mum

Jean ducks back behind the door

Len I know—I'll go and see her now.
Pauline Why don't you get a shower first. She's waited a long time for this—a few more minutes won't matter.
Len You're right. (*He kisses her on the cheek*)

Len goes out to the changing rooms. Pauline stands holding the side of her face for a moment then goes to the club-house. Jean comes in from the kitchen

Jean Oh no—not now ... why does he do this to me now when I've made my mind up. (*She walks around thinking*)

Ray comes in from the kitchen with her case

Ray I've got your case—come on, quick while there's no-one about. Let's go.
Jean (*looking at him*) It's too late.
Ray No, it's not. We can be in London by ten.
Jean No, Ray. London's too late. (*She takes her case from him*)
Ray What's happened?
Jean I think I still love him.
Ray You didn't fifteen minutes ago.
Jean He needs me.
Ray He's got a funny way of showing it!
Jean I'm sorry, Ray.
Ray So am I—if you're ever in the capital, look me up.

He bends to kiss her on the cheek but she turns and moves away

So this is how it ends, is it?
Jean Please don't be bitter.
Ray I'm not, I'm just confused. (*Going to her*) Jean! (*He puts his hand on her shoulder*)
Jean Ray—if you love me, just go.

Ray slowly takes his hand away and walks to the kitchen door

Ray (*turning*) Here's looking at you, kid. (*He smiles at her*)

Ray exits

Doc comes in from the kitchen a few seconds later

Doc That was Ray, wasn't it?
Jean (*upset*) Yes.
Doc Is he going?
Jean Yes.
Doc Doesn't he want a drink?
Jean No, he's driving.
Doc A very sensible man.
Jean (*getting more upset*) Yes, yes he is.
Doc Where's the captain?
Jean He's having a shower.
Doc I have a confession to make.
Jean There's a lot of it about.
Doc This team we're playing—I know who they are.
Jean (*not interested*) Really?
Doc Yes, it's the England ladies team. They're on a tour of Yorkshire before they go to Australia to take on their ladies team.
Jean Why didn't they say who they were.
Doc No-one's going to play a team of ladies and risk getting beaten. So they don't tell anyone who they are, they just turn up like today.

Jack comes in from outside drinking a pint of beer, followed by Duncan

Jack I'm soaked through. (*He drinks his pint down*) On inside as well as outside. (*He gives Duncan his empty glass*) I'm going for shower.
Duncan What's this?
Jack That's right kind of you. I'll have a pint of Yorkshire for when I come out.

He goes out to the changing room as Pauline comes in from the club-house

Pauline (*excitedly*) Mom! I've been talking to their captain—you'll never guess who they really are!
Jean They're England's ladies' cricket team.
Pauline You guessed!
Jean Ay, with a little help from Doc.
Pauline Bet you can't guess the next bit.
Jean Pauline, I'm not a politician, I don't have to guess.
Pauline (*excitedly*) They're going on a tour of Australia and you won't believe it——
Jean I won't if you don't tell me.
Pauline They want me to go with them to look after the kit.
Jean What!
Pauline You know—make sure it's washed, repaired and ready for use— apparently the girl who normally does it is pregnant. Isn't it great and they're going to pay me. Can you believe it, getting paid to go to Australia!
Jean I'm not letting you go there.

Pauline Why not?
Jean Because it's full of Australian men—what will your dad say?
Pauline It doesn't matter—I'm going.

There is a big scream from Len in the changing room

Jean See, you've upset him.

Jack comes out from the changing rooms with just a towel wrapped around him

Jack Doc, come quick! It's Len—I think he's broken his leg.
Doc How?
Jack He got in the shower and slipped on this. (*He hands Doc something*)
Doc (*looking*) It's a loo block.

Everyone looks at Duncan

Duncan He told me to put them everywhere!
Doc Not in the showers, idiot!

They all run into the changing room

From the club-house is heard everyone else singing "On Ilkley Moor Bar Tat"

CURTAIN

FURNITURE AND PROPERTY LIST

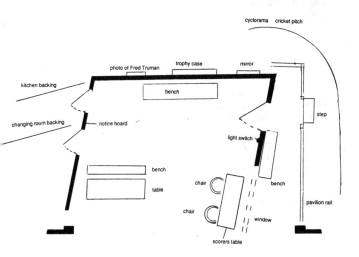

ACT I

Scene 1

On stage: Scoring table beside the window
 Large table
 Mirror
 Bench
 Hooks on wall. *On them*: cricket bat
 Chairs

Personal: **Pauline:** gherkin
 Billy: practical torch in jacket pocket, pavilion keys
 Ray: letter in pocket
 Len: pavilion keys

Scene 2

Strike: Gherkin

Re-set Cricket bat

Off stage Hand roller **(Billy)**
 Battered grass box **(Len)**
 Buckled wheel **(Ray)**

Personal: Shopping bag. *In it:* loo blocks **(Jean)**
Kit-bag **(Len)**
Shoe with loose heel **(Jean)**
Cravat **(Len)**
Contact lenses **(Doc)**
Stocking **(Jean)**
Handkerchief **(Doc)**
Car keys **(Pauline)**
Coin **(Mary)**

ACT II

SCENE 1

Set: Score book on score table
Len's cricket bat, gloves and pads
Duncan's bat and pads

Off stage: Strap-on box **(Jack)**
Cricket bat **(Jack)**
Crash helmet **(Ray)**

Personal: **Duncan:** bandage

SCENE 2

Re-set: **Len's** bat and gloves on bench (*or other convenient location*)

Set: Empty plates and cups, with one piece of celery, on table, Umpire's coat on the back of a chair. *In the pocket*: a cricket ball

Off stage: Tray **(Jean)**
Ball **(Jack)**
Case **(Ray)**
Loo block **(Jack)**

Personal: **Duncan:** large bandage
Ray: teatowel, rubber gloves, apron
Jean: key
Len: shampoo bottle (*in his pocket*), keys, £10 note
Alice: wrist-watch

LIGHTING PLOT

Practical fitting required: pendant light with bare bulb

Interior. The same scene throughout

ACT I, SCENE 1

To open: Dim moonlight

Cue 1	**Billy** switches on the light *Snap on property and general lighting*	(Page 1)
Cue 2	Car headlights flash across the window *Headlights pan across quickly*	(Page 4)
Cue 3	**Billy** runs over to the light switch and turns if off *Snap off property and general lighting, leaving dim moonlight*	(Page 4)
Cue 4	**Billy:** "... turned off the road." *Headlight effect visible through window*	(Page 4)
Cue 5	Headlights shine right in the window *Headlight effect strong, lighting room*	(Page 4)
Cue 6	**Ray** puts the light on *Snap on practical and general lighting*	(Page 4)
Cue 7	**Len** switches the lights to the pavilion off *Snap off property and general lighting, leaving dim headlight effect*	(Page 9)
Cue 8	They drive off *Headlights disappear*	(Page 9)
Cue 9	**Billy** switches the light on *Snap on practical and general lighting*	(Page 9)
Cue 10	**Billy** switches off the light *Black-out*	(Page 9)

ACT I, SCENE 2

To open: Afternoon interior effect with light coming through the window

No cues

ACT II, SCENE 1

To open: Afternoon interior effect

No cues

ACT II, SCENE 2

To open: Late afternoon interior

Cue 11. **Jean:** "A son."   (Page 47)
          Begin gradual dimming to signify approaching rain outside

EFFECTS PLOT

ACT I

Cue 1   **Billy:** "... in the morning for the game."   (Page 1)
Water drops through the roof on to Pauline.

Cue 2   **Pauline:** "... they kick me out."   (Page 3)
Water again drips through the roof on to Pauline

Cue 3   **Pauline:** "... learning something about cricket."   (Page 4)
Car heard approaching

Cue 4   **Billy:** "Under the table."   (Page 4)
*Car draws up, engine is switched off; 2 car door slams; footsteps
approaching the door*

Cue 5   **Pauline** and **Billy** crawl around one end of the table   (Page 5)
A noise from off DL

Cue 6   **Billy:** "Shh Hang on."   (Page 9)
*Sound of a car trying to start, on the third attempt it starts and
drives away*

Cue 7   **Len:** "... it doesn't happen again."   (Page 13)
Rumbling of roller, off

Cue 8   **Duncan:** "No, listen."   (Page 14)
The rumbling comes closer

Cue 9   **Doc.:** "... that does sound serious."   (Page 17)
Sound of a lawn mower trying to start, off

Cue 10   **Doc.:** "... hundreds of shoulders."   (Page 18)
Sound of a lawn mower trying to start, off

Cue 11   **Len** sits on the chair   (Page 18)
The mower tries to start again, off. A bang off, as the mower is hit

Cue 12   **Sally:** "Only between overs."   (Page 21)
*Sound of the lawn mower starting up, off. Shouts and screams. A
crash, followed by a loud bang*

ACT II

Cue 13   **Jean:** "... time for foreigners."   (Page 30)
Clapping, off

Cue 14   **Doc.:** "She'll kill him!"   (Page 35)
Sound of a ball being hit hard, off

Cue 15   **Len:** "... shampoo does for the ball."   (Page 43)
Noise, off

MADE AND PRINTED IN GREAT BRITAIN BY
LATIMER TREND & COMPANY LTD PLYMOUTH

MADE IN ENGLAND